The Artist's Eye:
BRIDGET RILEY

AN EXHIBITION OF NATIONAL GALLERY PAINTINGS SELECTED BY THE ARTIST

28 June – 31 August 1989
The National Gallery, London

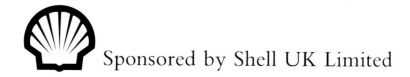

Sponsored by Shell UK Limited

The Artist's Eye: Bridget Riley: an exhibition of National Gallery Paintings selected by the artist.
1. European paintings, 1500–1800–Catalogues
I. Riley, Bridget, *1931–*
759.94'074

ISBN 0–947645–50–0

Front cover: detail from *Bacchus and Ariadne* by Titian
Back cover: *Bridget Riley*, photograph by David Dilley

Exhibition coordinated by Michael Helston
Exhibition designed by Herb Gillman
Catalogue designed by Roger Huggett

Printed and bound in Great Britain by W. S. Cowell Ltd

Robert Kudielka is Professor of Aesthetics and Philosophy of Art at the Hochschule der Künste, Berlin

Bridget Riley is represented by the Mayor Rowan Gallery, 31a Bruton Place, London W1

Erratum
The two pictures by Poussin have been transposed.
The *Adoration of the Shepherds* should appear opposite p.33 and the *Triumph of Pan* opposite p.35.

Director's Foreword

The history of art has been on the whole a black and white affair. Scholars and critics have of necessity worked from images that could be carried back to the study. Comparison and classification, analysis and explication all presuppose portable images, which until very recently meant engravings or black and white photographs. Not surprisingly, the history that results is predominantly one focused on subject matter and those qualities such as line and composition which survive reproduction.

In this year's *Artist's Eye* exhibition, Bridget Riley shows that where it is possible to arrange pictures themselves to tell the story, another history becomes apparent – a history that depends on colour and on succeeding artists' response to its use by the masters over many generations.

This *Artist's Eye* is in fact a historical argument, using the pictures as evidence. We hope that our visitors will be able to read the argument with the pictures in front of them, and that the resonances and echoes identified here will accompany the pictures when they return to their usual neighbours at the end of the summer.

The mounting of this exhibition has placed a considerable burden on my colleagues in the Gallery, and in particular on Peter Brett and his team, Herb Gillman, Michael Helston, Jean Liddiard, Alistair Smith and Lucy Trench. On behalf of all at the Gallery, I would like to thank them for responding so cheerfully to the challenges.

In conclusion, we would all wish to thank Shell UK Limited for their continuing and generous support of this series. We believe that these annual re-arrangements and the accompanying catalogues allow our visitors to get to know their pictures better and to see them in truer perspective. We are profoundly grateful to Shell UK Limited for making it possible.

Neil MacGregor
Director

Sponsor's Foreword

This is the fourth in the series of *Artist's Eye* exhibitions sponsored by Shell. We have been particularly proud to be involved in a project which allows distinguished artists to share with the public their personal choice of pictures from the National Gallery. Bridget Riley's selection makes an exciting and stimulating exhibition.

Bob Reid
Chairman and Chief Executive
Shell UK Limited

Acknowledgements

It is an honour to be invited to choose a group of paintings from such a collection as that of the National Gallery, one of the leading museums of the world. Having long been a visitor, I served for seven years as a Trustee and this provided experience on an institutional level. That period was a lesson in the power of works of art to affect peoples' lives. The serene spirit of the Gallery which the public enjoys emanates, of course, essentially from the paintings themselves; but this is supported by the dedication of the staff, from the warders to the Director, to their duty as preservers and caretakers in the *best* sense of the word.

In the preparation of this exhibition I am indebted to so many people who work in the Gallery that, though omission on paper may be inevitable, no kindness or assistance has passed unappreciated. First of all I would like to thank the Director, Neil MacGregor, for his enthusiasm and encouragement throughout. I would also like to thank Alistair Smith, the Head of Exhibitions, Michael Helston, the exhibition co-ordinator, Martin Wyld, the Head of Conservation, Jean Liddiard and Karen Bath in the Press Office, Lucy Trench and Sue Curnow in the Publications Department, Herb Gillman for his design for the exhibition, and Diana Davies, the Gallery editor. Colin Wiggins in the Education Department arranged the lecture series; Joan Lane, Carol McFadyen and Neil Aberdeen the accompanying video. I am more than grateful; it was a pleasure to work with all of them.

I would especially like to thank the sponsors, Shell UK Limited, without whose generosity none of these exhibitions could take place. Liberty of London Prints Limited made possible a specially dyed fabric for the Sunley Room. Roger Huggett designed all the graphic work and the catalogue with expertise. David Thompson's love of painting was an enormous asset in the production of the video. Finally my greatest debt is to Robert Kudielka for the time spent helping me with the text of this catalogue. It would simply not exist without his perception and tenacity.

Bridget Riley

Bridget Riley in conversation with Robert Kudielka

The Colour Connection

RK In what way does an artist's view of the collection differ from that of any other spectator or scholar visiting the National Gallery?

BR An artist sees the collection in much the same way as any vistor: he likes or dislikes certain paintings, and he benefits, like everybody, from some historical knowledge to help him bridge the gap to the art of the past. But an artist cannot help but be drawn, consciously or unconsciously, by interests particular to his work. He will be looking for points of contact through which his own problems may become a little clearer to him and, although no artistic intentions are ever the same, he may find comfort and encouragement in realising that certain fundamentals of making a painting remain fairly constant.

RK Is your present choice of painting governed by any specific theme? I remember that when, some time ago, you started to think about this exhibition you considered a different selection, focused on the 'perception of nature', including paintings by Constable, Monet, Seurat and others.

BR Yes, I did. But my own preoccupations have shifted a little and I have become more and more involved in the problems of plasticity – in that intangible quality which gives a painting its unique coherence. The artists whose work I have selected have each used colour in this particular way, as an element of construction.

RK That is an interesting idea, to associate colour with plasticity and construction. Is this the theme of the exhibition?

BR Yes. I very much hope that the seven great paintings shown in this exhibition – by Titian, Veronese, El Greco, Rubens, Poussin and Cézanne – will make it clear. These artists do not exactly form a tradition, but they connect with each other in many ways. Some of them even through personal contact, others solely through artistic judgement and appreciation. All of them however have one thing in common: they were interested in what it means to 'build' a painting in plastic terms.

1. Titian, *Bacchus and Ariadne*, 1520–2

RK So you start with Titian.

BR Yes. He is the first great colour painter. Giorgione may have seen some possibilities before him, but he seems to me to have thought that colour could stand by itself almost independently of drawing. It's an easy mistake to make – one gets excited by what one imagines will be a new freedom from old constraints. Titian, however, seems to have felt the need to reorientate the pictorial means as a whole rather than to abandon any one aspect in order to include colour more properly. A new and bold approach to composition was needed. The painting *Bacchus and Ariadne* shows him rising to this challenge in an amazing way.

RK Painted between 1520 and 1522, shortly after Titian's professional break-through with the *Assunta* of 1518, it marks the beginning of his mature work.

BR The painting is a shock, even today. We are so inured to the notion of shock in modern painting that we have come to suspect its validity. So one is reassured, while marvelling, by this painting's enduring capacity to startle. How is it done? The sheer volume of blue, and *what a blue*! You think at first that there is something wrong with the painting, that no one in his right mind could have hoped to get away with such an outrageous colour.

RK Some people still think that the pigment has changed, or might have been falsified by restoration.

BR I don't think that this is true. For instance, the red-brown tree in the top right is actually painted that colour. It's not an oxydisation of green. Modern conservation with its scientific analysis of pigments is able to ascertain such technical details.

RK It also tells us that the sky around Bacchus has lost some of its intensity through retouching.

BR But that doesn't affect the general scheme of the painting.

RK It's not a question of speculation about the original appearance of pigments or their state of preservation, is it?

BR No, that would be a red herring. How colours are identified doesn't discriminate sufficiently anyway. Our conception of the various hues has probably changed just as much over a period of time as they themselves have aged a little. It's irremediably obscure and quite irrelevant, provided that no great damage has happened to a painting. A painter would not be an artist if he were to pursue that sort of perfection. Late Monet, when his eyesight began to fail him, painted some of his most beautifully subtle canvases from the names on the tubes. To be able to do something like that was only possible because he knew through long experience that in the end it was the precision of relationships that counted.

RK And that, indeed, seems to be the crucial issue of *Bacchus and Ariadne*. Titian uses his blue with an abundance equal to its splendour. But how is it related? Deep blue was traditionally regarded as a difficult colour, even shunned by the Antique painters, because it seemed to threaten the coherence of imagery.

BR Titian however relates it in an extraordinary way. It seems as though he has taken this very hint from the past, and by pushing it to an extreme has turned it to his own ends. He makes no attempt to integrate the blue through other colours of equal intensity. With the exception of some of the reds, all the other hues – the greens and warm flesh tints – are very soft indeed.

RK But Titian enforces them as it were by endowing them with a particular dramatic role.

BR Exactly. He uses the complexity of his narrative to balance the blue. The action depicted and one's reaction as a spectator are linked in a special timescale invented by Titian for his subject. The pictorial time of *Bacchus and Ariadne* is a matter of instants. Straight after the saturated blue one sees the explosive force of the diagonal which cuts right across one's perception.

RK One can almost hear the maenad clashing the cymbals.

BR It's as though she says 'Now!'. This shows clearly one aspect of Titian's pictorial time.

RK Yes. After the immediacy of the first impact one discovers that this 'Now' is not a single moment in time. Titian has taken two successive episodes from the myth and turned them into one pictorial instant. His Antique sources, Catullus and Ovid, both tell the story of how Ariadne was abandoned by a faithless Theseus on the island of Naxos and of how Bacchus found her there. But each poet elaborates a different moment in the chain of events. Catullus depicts Ariadne in her grief, watching the ship disappear, when suddenly, 'from the other side', Bacchus makes his entry; and, in describing the god's following, he mentions nearly all the characters in the painting, including fakirs of some sort who were 'girding themselves with snakes'. Ovid in retelling the story a generation later in the eighth book of *Metamorphoses* shifts the emphasis to the encounter between the god and the mortal. To show Ariadne his love Bacchus transformed her diadem into an immortal constellation, the Crown, and through a slip of imagination Ovid places this next to another group of stars known in Antiquity as Ophiuchus, the Snake-Bearer.

BR   It would seem to be almost impossible to combine events of such fantastic diversity, but Titian succeeds because his way of building the painting equates to the poetics of mythology. Everything is bound together within a structure of analogies and contradictions. For instance, although the general character of the Bacchic retinue is disturbing, it also seems to be pervaded by a surprising sweetness which, like a gentle breeze, stirs the trees and, passing lightly over the whole, reaches its zenith in Bacchus – one of the most unforgettable images ever painted.

RK   His arrival traps Ariadne. Titian creates a sense of inevitability by directing the entire movement from which the god springs *against* the left to right reading of the painting.

BR   The encounter is rendered inescapable in every way. The space around Ariadne seems to have a depth all its own, a narrow corridor as opposed to the spreading lateral passage of the retinue, but at the end Bacchus awaits her too, in the crown of stars thrown into infinity. The combination of two such different types of space is an amazing device, hardly less so than the main contrast between the blue and the earth colours.

RK   But how is the unity of the painting achieved? So far we have been mainly speaking about oppositions, disruptions and counter-movements.

BR   I think that Titian achieves his unity by building the painting up according to those very factors which would seem most likely to tear it apart. What I mean is that he works through an intuitive logic of oppositions, distinguishing and simultaneously relating every inch of the canvas in a continuous web of contrasts, echoes, reversals, repetitions and inversions without either trying to form a unifying envelope or depending upon any simple common principle.

RK   Is this what you mean when you talk about 'building with colour'?

BR   Yes, but even when Titian considers the other properties of painting, such as form, he still thinks in terms of colour – that is to say, in contrasts and echoes. For example, Bacchus and Ariadne are clearly shown as complementary figures – and the girl with the cymbals is a secondary counter-image, her assured stance contrasting with that of Ariadne. Bacchus himself, with his open ease of movement, is the opposite of the twisted man struggling with his snakes. The very age of Silenus, who brings up the rear of the retinue, is reversed in the youth of the faun who leads it. The grace of Bacchus and the splendour of his gift to Ariadne are inverted, as it were, in comic distortion, by the barbaric offering of the clumsy satyr to the girl with the tambourine.

RK   So the relationships between the figures in the painting form a dramatic analogy to the colour structure.

BR   Yes, take the line of Bacchus' glance, it echoes the main diagonal. And this, which goes right across the canvas, dividing the painting into a blue area and a predominantly earth-red one, offers a sensitive edge across which these two main colours and their derivatives are reversed. Slivers of blue sparkle between the trees, the paler shades of the clouds are suggested in the dress of the girl with the tambourine, a full strong sky colour reappears in the skirt of the woman with cymbals, and at its most intense the blue culminates in Ariadne's clothes. Conversely, the reds at their earthiest and heaviest are reserved for the snake-bearer, who sets off a major colour echo in the autumnal tree above. Shifting hue, the reds travel down to Bacchus, where the magenta cloak and the flesh tints, quite soft colours in themselves, acquire almost full chromatic force by being isolated against the blue. Finally, the reds reach their most brilliant exponent in the vermilion of Ariadne's scarf, set against the blue of her dress.

RK   How about the clear yellow cloth below? It seems almost arbitrary at first glance.

BR   It has a sort of *repoussoir* role, putting the strong red and blue contrast of Ariadne's clothes into a relative position by introducing a third tension and at the same time strengthening the greens. So cunningly does Titian build his colour that this surprising addition is immediately absorbed into the whole canvas by his placing a few patches of yellow sunlight in the landscape above.

RK   This is a fascinating way of looking at the painting. But don't you think that it hampers or even impedes the reading of the image?

BR   No, how could it? Titian goes way beyond simply illustrating a mythological tale: he offers us a new way of experiencing it by transforming it into a purely pictorial event controlled by plastic considerations.

RK   What do you mean by plastic considerations?

BR   By plastic I mean that which hangs between the cognitive reading of an image and its perception. If one looks at the painting there is clearly a gap between the mythic illusion which one can 'read' and the immediacy of the sensations one experiences through the sense of sight. Titian uses the archaic imagery as a veil through which he creates an intangible web of organised sensations within the painting. The content of this web is as removed from the arcane quality of the myth as it is superior to mere decoration.

RK   But how is this brought about?

BR   By working with this 'between' as a primary consideration. That means that X and Y, say, are less important in themselves than the relationships they give rise to. Titian uses various structural particularities of colour for just this purpose. Whatever you see never exists simply and solely by itself, as an isolated sign or symbol, but by playing its part within a context in which relatedness as such is of the first importance.

RK   You mean that it is the quality of the relationships within the work which constitutes the plastic character of the painting, its 'hanging between'? Cézanne defined colour as 'the place where our brain and the universe meet', and he demonstrated his answer to this challenge with a famous gesture – that of joining both hands together with all the fingers firmly interlocked.

BR   Titian's web is certainly not as tight. He can afford to have celebrated mythic figures such as Bacchus and Ariadne standing out of the pictorial fabric. But if one looks at the grouping of the other figures it is very revealing how far the primacy of relationship is pushed. There are very few figures indeed which are complete in themselves – shoulders overlap, legs seem to belong to several creatures, hidden limbs acquire illogical substitutes – so that, in effect, figures are broken up and reassembled in a new plastic anatomy which I call to myself 'collective figuration'.

RK   It's the beginning of the colour structure he developed over a period of fifty years. Whereas in *Bacchus and Ariadne* Titian still relies upon certain

2. Veronese, *The Adoration of the Kings*, 1573

Fig. 1. Titian, *The Death of Actaeon*, c. 1560–75

Fig. 2. Titian, *The Pesaro Madonna*, 1519–26

VERONESE

formal places for colour, he later goes on in works such as the *Death of Actaeon* in the National Gallery to fabricate pictorial unity almost entirely out of a continuously shifting modulation of a group of colours, carefully chosen and balanced for this purpose.

BR And that is the enigma of his achievement.

RK Though such extreme solutions could not directly give rise to the Venetian tradition of colour as we know it.

BR One cannot go from high point to high point, as Pascal says. It was Paolo Veronese who took the necessary steps to translate Titian's innovations into comprehensible principles. Titian is the kind of painter whom one can only admire. For practical guidance it is better to turn to Veronese. At least this is how both Delacroix and Cézanne understood it.

RK It is a pattern of appreciation which seems to have conditioned Veronese's own response. When this Paolo Caliari from Verona arrived in Venice in 1555, he encountered a Titian at the height of his powers. But instead of succumbing to the influence of Titian's mature work he found his own measure through relating to an earlier phase of the master's development. It seems to have been paintings such as the *Pesaro Madonna* from the early 1520s which were to provide his own starting-point.

BR The connection is clear when one looks at the *Adoration of the Kings*. There is a similar diagonal development of the colours, articulated by the drapery, set against a massive piece of architecture.

RK But obviously the colour is notated in a different key. The hues are less brilliant and a specific tone, a kind of medium lightness, seems to prevail throughout the painting.

BR I don't think it is a different key but the use of a coherent colour envelope as such which makes Veronese's approach so different from Titian's. His colour is based on a mid-tone level which is used in two ways, as an actual grey and as the abstract pitch towards which all hues relate. The grey must have been a wonderful silvery shade when first painted, and it probably related to the actual setting of the painting.

RK Unfortunately the church of San Silvestro, for which this painting was made in 1573, was converted in the nineteenth century in such a way that the original placement is no longer available. But it is very likely that the grey of the stone together with the subdued church light provided an architectural setting perfectly tuned to that inflected, indirect light, *le temps gris*, which Delacroix was to regard as the most favourable condition for the observation of colour in nature.

BR Veronese uses this grey in two ways, as an armature for the colour structure and for wrapping around all his figures, bathing the whole in its light. Quite naturally the principal hues compatible to such a milieu are very unstable ones. There are no central blues, reds or yellows – they would break the grey envelope. Instead he has tangential derivatives, colours which are tipped and slanted towards the tertiaries: towards turquoise or lime green, mauve or earth red, ochre or orange.

RK The approximation of all colours to a common mid-tone, emphasised by a pervasive grey, destabilises the chromatic identities. This is a strategy which you have often employed in your own work, as I remember, in order to release the perceptual energy of colour. But instability as such, without a structural counterpoint, can easily result in visual inertia. How does Veronese articulate this diffuse, spatially rather shallow blend of colours?

BR By interlocked diagonals – powerful lines which zigzag sharply down and across the painting. The restrictions in any movement back and forth imposed by the shallow range of colour space are compensated for by twisting the dynamics of recession *flat*, as it were.

RK So a device, found by Giorgione and developed by Titian, is elaborated in an almost systematic fashion. In the absence of the projective pull of perspectival space, diagonal vectors activate the painting. In the *Adoration* this structural reading is literally illuminated by the shaft of light which singles out Mary, in a long falling diagonal, as the focus of the painting.

BR If Titian's diagonal is a bold thrust – Veronese's is as gentle as a silken cord. Understated, almost transparent, this beam of light is still strong enough to swing the entire movement of the *Adoration* in a slow arc – like the clapper of a great bell.

RK That's a beautiful simile. It encompasses both the linear organisation and the development of colour. The amplitude of the swing is indicated by straight formal echoes of the falling diagonal in the bottom left and the top right corner, whereas the rising sequence of the worshippers, paralleled by the angle of the roof of the stable, introduces a sense of spatial reverberation. The sound of this bell, however, seems to be carried by colour.

BR   It is made up of 'weights'. Each of the principal hues is laid out first in clear bold statements. Take the reds, for instance. The heaviest accent is obviously the big coat of the kneeling king, although it is hard to say exactly which sort of red it is – whether the warm or cool variant is dominant. In the bulk of the brocade an orange-red mid-tone is played against a lower, cooler red which is extended into the blue-magenta lining of the epaulettes. Smaller in area but more brilliant, the orange red reappears in the headdress of the man behind, a culminating point, which is echoed in the breeches of the king with the golden cloak. The orange-red theme is concluded in the dull burnt orange of Joseph's clothes, circling round the surprisingly light mauve-magenta of Mary's dress.

RK   And what about the shadowed attendant on the extreme left?

BR   He plays a similar role in the red movement to that of Joseph. If Joseph is the chromatically subdued end of the red arc, the attendant is the beginning: a low-key obscure prelude.

RK   But there is also a slighter extension, a barely visible pink-magenta thread, which is woven into the fabric of the painting. It can be traced in the shine of the horsemen's armour, in the sparkle of the censer carried by the black king, as well as in the appliqué of his trousers. This peripheral flicker travels via the light grey horses in the background right up to the middle of the painting, where it is substantiated by the lilac belt of the man with the red turban. It continues in the pink decoration of the luggage and eventually dissolves into a luminous orange-violet reflection in the horseman standing by the stable.

BR   If you look carefully you can see the same treatment in all the other colours. It shows his method of working in the studio. First, the big areas would have been blocked in by Veronese and his studio assistants – in this case, his brother and his two sons. Then, as the painting developed, smaller marks of the same or closely related colours would have been added across other areas. Trimmings, trappings, light falling and shadows would all offer pretexts for extending and, as you say, weaving the colours in and through the painting.

RK It may be a simple working procedure, but it is also the clue to his magic of suggestion. Whatever he wants to indicate – light, a particular texture or plain local colour – seems to be primarily a question of how far he would transform these basic blocks. Thus, the very same ochre could remain as an inconspicuous earth or flesh colour, or be treated to the most incredible permutations. It could be converted into the airy texture of the plumes or into an even flow of light; it could be raised to the appearance of 'real gold', like in the cloak of the kneeling king, and it could be played down to the bland sensation of animal skin, as in the ox directly opposite. But sometimes, and most perplexing to us, he didn't bother with elaboration at all, like in the hand of that red king, which seems to be proof of the claim of his detractors that he could not paint hands at all . . .

BR Yes – but that is of course nonsense! Veronese left this hand indistinct because it is *meant* to be ignored, to remain in half shadow. His sort of reasoning doesn't go in for accuracy in detail but for a collective truth. Look at the king's arm and the cloak of his page. They form together one red shape, but Veronese separates the figures in a way that is really remarkable. Instead of delineating the sleeve he distinguishes it from the cloak by a clear touch of green which is only connected perceptually to the green tunic of the man with a red headdress behind him. It's a plastic invention.

RK Yes. It is one of those instances through which Veronese delighted the protagonists of modern painting in the nineteenth century. Delacroix admitted candidly, as René Piot recalls, that he had discovered the law of contrast in Veronese's *Marriage at Cana* in the Louvre before Chevreul even started his scientific researches. He saw it in the collar of the page on the left of the painting, where the actual yellow ochre gives a golden sensation by virtue of a stroke of dull violet.

BR But I don't think Veronese had the modern idea of complementaries. It's the totality of colour that matters to him. The little green mark is one of smaller traces of the green movement. There are others nearby, such as the olive touches in the tassel and lining of the big collar worn by the silver-white figure in the foreground. They help to alleviate the weight of the greens in much the same way as the pink marks do the reds. In fact, the passaging of the greens almost mirrors that of the reds. Beginning with the cloak of the black king, a huge green block of darkly saturated olive and emerald, it is raised to maximum brilliance in the tunic of the figure in the background: a wonderfully clear fresh green which equates to the intense red of his turban. Aided by those smaller traces, it then finds its way to the opposite cool end of the green scale, turquoise, in Mary's cloak – rounded off with one last touch of olive in the lining.

RK But surely this does not account for the entire green theme?

BR No. It can be perceived in reverse; and probably this is the more significant direction. As a turquoise blue it starts with the sky, travels down in the wings of the angels and arrives at the figure of Mary as the colour of her cloak. There it splits into blue and green. As blue it gains prominence, thanks to colour contrast, in the golden brocade of the kneeling king, while the green tendency is extended to the moor's cloak.

RK And again, this cadence seems to be partially accompanied by a subdued counterpoint. If one looks closely at the garland of angels flung around the shaft of light, one discovers in the wings of the two lower cherubinetti, apart from distinct traces of green, also portions of a very dark blue and magenta; and what is more, these nearly black tints recur in the clothes of the onlookers behind the beam. They seem to provide a kind of 'colour shadow' which adumbrates the emergence of the light blue and magenta in Mary's robe.

BR One could go on finding many more such surprising relationships and correspondences. Nothing seems to be arbitrary in Veronese's world; yet the colour unity appears so natural, that it may be hard to believe that it is deliberate.

RK This balance between ease and order must have been at the root of his legendary 'fame' which lasted right until the beginning of modern art. Veronese was the famous painter *par excellence*: much appraised as long as praise seemed to be the highest form of appreciating art. But he fell somewhat into oblivion when art became subject to methodical inter-pretation. Cecil Gould has said that the lack of proper art-historical studies on Veronese presents a task of 'alarming dimensions'. Why do you think this is so?

BR   It may have to do with the understanding of what I called 'plastic'. Veronese lays bare this web which hangs between perception and cognition more openly than Titian because he doesn't seem to be interested in expression. One can see that this could easily be misunderstood as 'decorative', in merely derogatory terms.

RK   The 'most gentle entertainment', *soauissimo trattenimento*, Ridolfi calls it, as opposed to the *eroica maestà* of Titian.

BR   Yes. But this gentleness or sweetness is not weak, or a lack of some vital artistic quality. It is a preferred detachment. A renunciation of what is loosely understood as expressiveness could perhaps have seemed to a sovereign spirit such as Veronese simply the setting aside of a distraction which would allow him greater freedom on a deeper level. His form of expression is purely plastic – *that's* what makes it so strong and enduring. And, I think, why it has meant so much to other painters over the centuries.

RK   It is certainly more complex than a quick glance can grasp. Only after a while one discovers, in the centre of the painting, a rough-hewn wooden pole, which in conjunction with the beam of the stable and the lintel of the architecture forms a gigantic veiled cross. The future is as much present in the momentary splendour of the *Adoration* as is the past, indicated by the ruins of the old temple tucked away behind the stable. There is a distinct sense of the poise of existence in Veronese. All aspects and characters of the painting seem to share a collective identity: each of them is specific, but none peculiar, isolated from the others; and the situation *in toto*, though a magic and unique event, is far from being charged with the glamour of the extraordinary.

BR   It's the actual reality of colour. One wonders, as one cannot with the Titian, why the painting is so familiar. It almost seems as though Veronese not only dealt with his own problem in painting but provided an insight which has reappeared again and again in canvases of different styles and periods. This insight would seem to be that beyond any identifying of subjects or any isolating of elements – such as, for instance, strong hues – the *whole* is regarded as the most important thing. And it's exactly at that point that colour plays a key role. One of colour's mysteries is that it can do two contradictory things at the same time: each individual hue can contribute to the overall sensation, and yet still remain itself.

RK Is it the painter's realisation of that inconceivable entity – the *colour* of colours?

BR Exactly.

EL GRECO

RK But what then about El Greco? Why did you include the *Expulsion of the Traders from the Temple* in your selection? He seems to be far from being a 'colourist': his space is torn up by vehement perspectives and his figures are shrouded in a dramatic chiaroscuro – devices which are, by all accounts, not sympathetic to colour.

BR That is true, but it's only part of the story. There is another side to Titian's understanding of colour. Apart from showing its subtle complexities he also saw the need for a certain toughness to push out its boundaries. It shows the breadth and strength of the Venetian tradition that it could sustain a wide range of temperaments and controversial interpretations. El Greco, an expressionist in our terms, may rock the colour boat through Mannerist distortions and intense religious feeling. But in doing so he adds an important new force to colour's armoury – and that is *rhythm*. Take the strong projection of space which you mention. It is certainly there, but it is interesting how the perspective is handled. Instead of one, there are two vanishing points: the main one directly to the right of Christ and an eccentric one to the far right. Being crooked or skew-whiff, they counteract the very focus they promise and, through that, provide the lateral tension of the rhythm which he builds across the canvas.

RK The whole composition seems to reverberate with oblique correspondences. The equilibrium of the central symmetry swings between the agitated traders on one side and the passive observers on the other. And again, *this* balance is set off - skew-whiff, as you would say – through the

3. El Greco, *The Expulsion of the Traders from the Temple, c.* 1600

dynamic figure of Christ in the centre foreground and his counterpart, the abstracted girl in the far distance on the right. But what role does colour play in all this?

BR   It works in two ways. Unlike Veronese, El Greco makes a clear distinction between the brilliance of his strong colours and a pervasive, liverish, putty grey which seems to form a sort of bed for the accents of the painting. One function of this strange grey is to bridge extremes: between lights and darks, warms and cools and, very ingeniously, between the main yellow-blue contrast. Its other role is to draw together the flesh colours and the stone of the architecture.

RK   The correspondence is almost metaphorical – and strongly reminiscent of late Titian. Do you remember the *Pietà* in the Accademia in Venice? There you have a similarly mysterious equation between stone and flesh. It is known that on his way from Crete to Spain El Greco stayed in Venice between 1565 and 1570, and worked as a studio assistant to Titian. Although in formal terms he owes more to Tintoretto and Bassano, his colour sense seems to have been formed, if only partially, by that impalpable grey which permeates late Titian's colour.

BR   But only partially. El Greco tears the grey apart by shattering his colours across the picture plane. These outcrops of colour – like highly-lit rocks – are then interrelated through a kind of cross-over thinking. One can see it most clearly in the blue and yellow of the pair of conversing figures in the right foreground: the colours are inverted, remaining almost equal in quantity, in the yellow and blue of the two people on the left of Christ who flinch away from him. The man in the yellow cloth and the woman falling backwards are re-formed in a new abstract unit, a colour synthesis, which provides a key to the plastic structure of the painting. Quite apart from the actual 'story', colour re-defines the figuration in such a way that axes of visual tension are created which form a rhythmic framework for the figure of Christ.

RK   The build-up is so complex, one layer of devices upon another, that it can only be explained by the steady refinement which El Greco has invested in it. There are at least a dozen versions of the same theme, spread over a period of thirty years, preceding and surrounding the present composition. Here Christ is placed in the centre of the action, as one would expect; yet, he also seems to be completely set apart from the other figures. The magenta of his robe is a unique accent, the only red besides the subordinate orange in the waistcoat of the trader in the left foreground. He alone incorporates the full tonal contrast of the painting, carrying the darkest shadow in his blue coat and exposing the highest tonal pitch in the glittering highlight down his right side.

BR One can certainly see him as a single figure, but he is also the quintessence of the whole painting. His gesture is drawn through the responses of those around him. The action doesn't exist, and yet, it is almost palpably there. The swing of his upraised arm is described in the curve of his disciples watching the event, and the stroke of the flail is anticipated in the exposure of the bodies which will receive it. The whole painting spins around the vortex of this movement which is not literally depicted – which is only *virtual*, implied in the actual structure.

RK Do you think it was this virtual 'energy and motion' that attracted Pollock to El Greco when he made his copies after reproductions in the 1930s?

BR It may have been. There is a free-floating rhythm in the painting which seems to hang there, self-contained, almost dancing – and quite flat. El Greco places the eye-level very high, tips the foreground down – emphasising this through the overturned table – and, further aided by the *repoussoir* figure bending over on the left, he pushes the whole lower half of the painting back.

Fig. 3. Pollock, studies after El Greco, 1937–8

RK The suspension accounts for the surprisingly serene presence of the painting. Although severe, the interference of Christ is not shown as any Herculean labour of purging the stables, as it were, nor is there any trace of bitterness or condemnation. While the flail is about to strike, the girl on the far right calmly counts the money in her hand, an innocent accomplice in the machinations of the world. Two reliefs in the background architecture confirm the symbolic meaning of the incident which El Greco has conveyed so superbly. The left one shows the first expulsion, the Expulsion from Paradise, whereas the right one, representing the Sacrifice of Isaac, implies an enigmatic promise of redemption, based on the analogy of a father willing to sacrifice his son.

BR   I am very much aware that this painting cannot be fully appreciated by concentrating on its colour alone. That is true, of course, of all paintings, but especially so in El Greco. He aspires to a different spiritual reality than that offered by colour, although it probably could not have been realised so powerfully *without* colour. One could see him at one end of a scale, the other end of which might be Rubens.

RUBENS

RK   The *Allegory of Peace* is indeed another world. Everything there appears in a different light.

BR   And what a wonderful light! If you first catch sight of the canvas from some distance there seem to be big bright cloud-like shapes sailing through it. They turn out to be the bodies which are the luminous heart of the painting – there's nothing lighter anywhere else. In a sense these flesh colours generate the internal radiance of Rubens' masterpiece.

RK   As if flesh were turned into a source of light instead of being equated with stone. But how is it done?

BR   It's brought about through a spectrum of colours – there's no other way. Certain colours placed in certain juxtapositions can generate a sort of light, as Seurat knew later on. Rubens isn't in any position, though, to base his procedure on an analysis of light. He draws on physical suggestion instead. Skin is a very complex colour compound, and subject to an infinite variety of inflections. Look at that great long back on the left. The surface is a little worn, and that enables one to see parts of the colour structure more clearly. There are yellows, violets, pinks and greens, all raised to a very high key indeed. Being so pale they would not be able, just by themselves, to bring about this extraordinary brilliance. But in a context of extension they gain sufficient strength to do so. All the strong shades of yellow, violet, green and red, which appear and reappear in drapery, act as exponents of those fugitive tints. The colour is orchestrated with such a resonance that even the highest notes can carry its theme.

RK   An ingenious device, which has influenced generations of painters right up to Delacroix and Renoir. It was certainly prepared for by the role which the flesh colours had assumed in the understanding of Venetian colourism. But this tradition alone does not sufficiently explain Rubens' innovation, as his earliest

4. Rubens, *Allegory of Peace*, 1629–30

version of the *Judgement of Paris* in the National Gallery shows. In that painting he still seems to follow a common studio recipe of the Antwerp school – creating a rather uneasy red and green glow in the nudes. After his return from Italy this distortion quickly subsides, but it was not only enriched experience which precipitated his mature solution. In 1613 a friend of his, Franciscus Aguilonius, published *Six Books on Optics*, to which Rubens contributed the illustrations. It is generally assumed that he also had a share in the revolutionary thesis included in this work: that all colours can be deduced from three primaries – blue, red and yellow.

BR Perhaps Rubens was the first painter to have a distinct concept of the totality of colour. The best proofs of this are the copies after Titian which he made in Spain in 1629, shortly before the *Allegory of Peace*.

RK They all show – like the portrait of Charles V now in the Courtauld – a remarkable shift towards red, yellow and blue. Rubens understands the colour unity of a painting generally in terms of those three primaries, through which it can be *produced*.

BR And then, he turns them into a source of light. The painting is divided into two parts. Colour and brilliance enter in force from the left and take over the entire foreground; the rest is dark, an annihilation of both these qualities. But this darkness is not entirely negative: it has a role – one of pushing the whole composition right up to the front of the picture plane.

RK In other words, there is no plain chiaroscuro, no continuous modulation from light to dark. Colour and light play their own theme against a dark background which is only momentarily broken up by the amazing passage of blue sky. Otherwise the space is extremely frontal, reducing the possibilities of organisation quite considerably.

BR Rubens uses the most celebrated gift of the Venetian tradition, after colour: the diagonal. It recurs time and again as a formal agent aiding and abetting the organisation of colour. As often, Rubens goes from corner to corner. Two huge diagonals cross the canvas. One rises from the back foot of the entry figure on the left, runs up through the figure of Peace, or more precisely, along the line of the red cloth over her lap, continues through Mars' shield and out through the phantoms in the top right. The other falls from the woman with the tambourine, via the satyr's wreath of leaves, the cornucopia and the

Fig. 4. Pollock, study after Rubens'
Allegory of Peace, 1937–8

putto's head, and ends in the outstretched leg of the girl in gold.

R K   But there is obviously an explicit preference for the downward movement, which Pollock has grasped instinctively in his little copy of the painting. Minerva's strong arm determinedly pushes away Mars, who is drawn by the Fury of War, as if to protect the gentle gathering of light and colour against the threat that looms over it. Placed in the centre of the painting, this decisive gesture distinguishes the painting from the *Allegory of War* in the Palazzo Pitti, where the rising diagonal is turned into a fatal force of destruction.

B R   It's more a matter of balance, I think. If a falling diagonal were to be so exaggerated as the rising one is in the *Allegory of War*, it would probably appear flaccid. Rubens establishes a relationship between these opposing directions by building up a grid or lattice around which he can twist or through which he can pour his colours. Do you see the two red diagonals echoing one another? The first starts from the heavy backcloth in the top left, falls down beside Peace, floods into her drapery and finishes below the cornucopia. The second begins in the big fold hanging down from the tree, travels through Mars' cloak and ends in small touches of red in the landscape on the right.

R K   So he actually repeats and extends the axial relationship throughout the painting – in much the same way as he proceeds with his colour theme – providing compartments in which he can allocate its development. Is that what you mean by 'lattice'?

B R   Yes. Take the beautiful yellow gold. Making use of his lattice he twines a long curving garland of yellows down and across the painting. Sometimes it enters into this or that relationship with different colours, and at other times it plays out a virtually independent movement. But in either case, although it may be hair, metal, fruit, clouds or skin, Rubens disposes it quite logically.

R K   According to which logic?

B R   That is is difficult to say. It's certainly *not* one concerned with 'substance'. To go back to the yellow. It seems to be the most important colour of all, and yet there is not a great deal of actual yellow in the painting. So it must be the question of an implicit quality. At its most brilliant, in the lightest parts of the bodies, it is indistinguishable from the sensation of light itself, before Rubens moves it into greens. The satyr carries the main modulations: bronzed and

Fig. 5. Rubens, *Allegory of War*, 1638

burnished by juxtapositions, all the inflections are there – ochres, olives, browns – which taken together yield a radiance comparable to that of the two women. As a lodestone of the yellow movement this figure is flanked by two surprising adjuncts in the chain of colour cadences. One is the treasure carried by the entry figure . . .

RK   A personification of Plenty, according to the attributes accompanying her.

BR   In the golden bowl and vessels the hues are warmer, lighter, more transparent. The other extension is the group of fruits offered in the cornucopia. Pale and opaque in the gourd, the yellows shift their character through the grapes towards turquoise. Picking up the reflection of the distant blue sky, these clusters form a little coda to the yellow development, which ends in the wings and the back of the putto. And just when one thinks that the variations are concluded the whole thing starts up again, with a counterthrust of clear yellow gold in the dress of the girl on the right setting off another chain of events: the shine of hair and skin, the blazing torch, the reflections in the armour, sunlight striking the clouds.

RK   The autonomy of the colour structure is very apparent. If one contrasts this painting with the Veronese, one is made aware of an important shift of emphasis. In the Rubens the plastic properties assume a significance of their own.

Fig. 6. Rubens, *Venus, Mars and Cupid*, 1629

POUSSIN

BR   But not in a decorative sense surely.

RK   No, his subject matter seems to be affected as well. It has long been acknowledged that the configuration of Peace and her child is directly related to the Dulwich painting of *Venus, Mars and Cupid*, where Venus feeds Cupid in the same playful manner. It's for Rubens specialists to decide what Venus and Cupid have in common with Peace and her Plutus child. But the parallel to the colour thinking is obvious. In Rubens' mind an image seems to be capable of carrying different meanings in much the same way as a colour theme may represent the most diverse objects. The significance of any entity or element is not determined by an external reference system, but is rendered within the context of painting.

BR   That sounds familiar! Does modern art start that early?

RK   The tendency is certainly borne out by the two Poussin paintings you have selected. Look at those Arcadian shepherds, dressed as though for a pagan festival rather than a biblical event. There is a sense of classical composure in the bacchanal which one would not associate with an orgiastic rite. Poussin presents a world which is so evidently a pictorial abstraction that it eludes any historical reference.

BR   That helps to account for his formality, which can be quite disconcerting if one rejects the type of invention in his paintings or if one doesn't understand the need for this extreme artifice. His work is not unlike grand opera, which can only be enjoyed by accepting its conventions.

RK   This may be the experience of Poussin today. But when he started to work in this manner there were no such conventions. He had to invent the rules himself. An amazing achievement, and even more so as it was in opposition to the course of development his own talent seemed to be following at the time. Poussin was a painter who was familiar with the life of the gutters. When first in Rome, although under the auspices of his humanist patron, he joined the ranks of the bravura painters for a while and indulged in such gross rhetorical excesses as the *Martyrdom of Saint Erasmus* and the *Massacre of the Innocents* – images of unbridled violence. But suddenly, between 1630 and 1631, he changed into that formidable pinnacle of order and control.

BR   Both the paintings I have selected are from the mid-1630s, so his work must have reached its classical form very quickly. Poussin probably had some sort of crisis, rather like Cézanne between 1869 and 1870, which set free a deeper creative self. Despite the widespread view to the contrary, it's often a rather uncouth or oddly intense temperament which excels in discipline and formality – in the arts at least.

RK   How would you describe the particular rules he invented for himself?

BR   They are very clear in the *Adoration of the Shepherds*. The way he uses his diagonals tells one a great deal about his reasoning. Those that recede in space are counteracted by those that lie parallel to the picture plane. There is a long passage projected back from Mary to the light in the distant sky, and the implicit line of this recession is simultaneously described by the completely flat diagonal of the shepherds bending down towards the child. The same thinking is even more apparent in the treatment of the architecture. The wall with the arch behind Mary is in a perspectival plane which is paralleled by the oblique angle of the roof drawn across the surface of the canvas. The end of the stable beam projecting towards us is illuminated by a patch of golden light virtually identical with that in the clouds behind it.

RK   The device is consistent, and what is more, the double reading is extended to the presentation of the figures. While their bodies are beautifully rounded, their drapery is treated in a different way. If one half-shuts one's eyes, one realises that the folds are generally registered in a light and dark contrast with very little gradation in between. Poussin simplifies tonal modelling to a light and dark alternation: the lighter parts provide for the most brilliant hues, the darker for subservient shades. Through this he can create a powerful colour structure independent of local values.

BR   And one sees a circular rhythm of colour. Ushered in by a sharp blue in the entry figure – who carries what amounts to the palette of the painting, a basket of fruits – it drops down to a contrasting orange qualified by pinks, tans, ochres and sage greens. Then, reaching an echoing blue around Christ and turning back through Mary's cloak and Joseph's yellow sleeve, it comes to an enigmatic stop, two onlookers in the shade . . .

RK   A fermata.

BR   . . . before returning to the opening note via the scene of the Revelation to the Shepherds, a small painting within the painting, removed in time and space.

RK   It's truly musical, isn't it? By suspending the weight of the two traditional

5. Poussin, *The Adoration of the Shepherds, c.* 1637

disciplines governing painting – architecture and sculpture – Poussin introduces a new affiliation of plastic thinking: the simile of music.

BR   Yes, the whole painting seems to be composed in a particular harmony. The colours of the rondo are carried on in a kind of serpentine movement. They are transposed into the pale yellows and grey blues of the sky and finally reassembled in the group of cherubs, a flurry of delicate tints carried by a perfectly poised cluster of diagonals.

RK   What about the blend of earth red, ochre and a bluish grey in the architecture?

BR   It's a beautiful composite colour – and perhaps the most important one in the entire canvas. Like a chord it reverberates throughout, modulated towards the blues, the earthy reds and yellow oranges in turn. It seems as though the equilibrium of the painting depends upon the range suggested by this colour.

RK   And one's emotional response as well. The mood of the *Adoration* is serene, jubilant and benign at the same time. As you know, Poussin was very much aware of the expressive character of his colour harmonies. In a famous letter to one of his patrons, Chantelou, he claimed that he employed different 'modes' of expression for different subjects. It's a reference to the Greek theory of music, but it can be very misleading if one tries to verify it in his work because there is no actual 'system' which he applies. But he nevertheless chooses his colour chords very carefully in relation to the character of the subject he is painting. Don't you think it is significant that in the *Adoration* he excludes that deep carmine which often figures so prominently in his religious paintings?

BR   I don't see how Poussin could have included that particular colour here. It would have upset the entire balance of the painting. But it is interesting that you mention it – plain red may not be physically painted in anywhere, but the sensation of redness is so strongly evoked by the colour chord that you sense it in every corner of the canvas.

RK   How would you then explain the difference of the *Triumph of Pan*? The actual colours seem to be very much the same: blues, earth reds, greens and yellows.

BR   They may be much the same, but they are used very differently. The painting has nothing to do with the sweetness a harmony may bring. One sees a display of frictions and facets. The colours are contrasted, red against green, blue against yellow, light against dark. The mellowness of a mid-tone pitch has been replaced by a full tonal gamut running from darkness to glitter.

6. Poussin, *The Triumph of Pan*, before 1636

Fig. 7. Poussin, study for a *Bacchanal*, c. 1640

Fig. 8. Poussin, studies for *The Triumph of Pan*, c. 1635–7

Fig. 9. After Giulio Romano, *The Triumph of Priapus*, engraving after the Master of the Die

RK It's a buoyant and exultant 'mode', and it seems to be based upon an increased emphasis on rhythm. If you compare the painting with a small crayon and bistre study for a *Bacchanal* in the Louvre, you can get a good idea of the tonal underpinning carrying this rhythm. By exaggerating and sharply accentuating the light and dark contrasts Poussin dismembers, as it were, all individual features in order to reconnect them in an overriding dynamic structure.

BR The little study certainly has a tremendous pace. But in the painting colour modulates and slows down that rhythm, allowing complex counter-movements to develop. The whole movement grows and fills out: the rhythm, no longer an even beat, becomes progressive.

RK You mean there is a left to right development in the painting?

BR It's not a simple, straightforward progression. The diagonal which runs down the mountain to Pan, along the arms of the nymph decorating him, to the little boy – who with great glee seems to be pushing the entire movement back – this diagonal both pulls and counters the collective development which builds up against it.

RK The general strategy seems to have been mapped out in an engraving after Giulio Romano which Poussin obviously used. Although much more lateral, frieze-like in organisation, with a plain central division, this simple image nevertheless contains an important clue to the sophistication of the *Triumph of Pan*. The relationship between the female faun touching the herm and the running man on the right side prefigures the reversal of the progressive movement which Poussin enacts through connecting the gesture of the nymph with that of the boy.

BR   Poussin pitches direction against counter-direction. In his preparatory studies one can see him pushing and pulling the image about, kneading it like dough. The engraving may be a good composition but it is not plastic. It depicts figures in motion: Poussin makes the entire scene move.

RK   The rhythm literally re-creates the bodies, giving rise to the most surprising instances of pictorial anatomy. As for 'collective figuration', look at this amazing entry group. The man with the fanfare who heralds the introduction of the opposite diagonal is firmly built into the physique of the other two figures surrounding the girl on the goat – joining them or being joined to them, whichever way you look at it. His left leg straightens out, as it were, the back of the kneeling man with the flower basket on his head, while his right leg is linked with that of the man holding the girl, whose other leg helps to support the goat. One could go on pointing out such plastic liberties throughout the whole group. But they alone would probably add up only to an entanglement of bodies, were it not for the decisive role colour plays in relocating identities.

BR   There is a lovely broad colour diagonal, which runs from the tip of the flower basket through the two nymphs up to the tambourine, turns, and, removed in space, travels back through the landscape and the sky. Cool and fresh, it is made up mainly of whites, blues and violets, accompanied by contrasting oranges and yellows. Apart from the drapery and the statue – ideal carriers for the boldest colour abstractions – the chain is linked through the pale shine of skin, its violet shadows and the blue haze of distance. The thrust of this diagonal is encircled by a twisted curve of earth reds, apricots, pinks, oranges and rosy colours. Poussin's collective figuration allows him to draw with colour a modulated sequence which begins with the kneeling man, curves up above the nymph on the goat, down below Pan, round the second nymph in lilac blue, and ends up in the fluttering drapery on the far right. This beautiful warm colour-form is punctuated by little clusters of sage greens, turquoises and yellow ochres, which appear as wreaths, hair and iridescent silk.

RK   If one adopts this way of looking, the notorious 'Poussin barrier' quickly vanishes. Most people sense, I think, that they are not meant to recognise well-worn sentiments and clearly identifiable facts in these highly abstract compositions; and this suspension of direct cognition is part of that barrier. In looking at the painting one is instantly made aware of a distinct diversion in perceiving it, like listening to a musical overtone . . .

BR But it's not an overtone! In this instance the musical simile is misleading. It's just the opposite. That curious, elusive quality you are referring to is the *substance* of the painting, the entire body of relationships which Poussin has so carefully fabricated.

RK Yes, but the fabric does not simply serve representation. It subverts, as it were, the connection between the eye and the mind by diverting and redirecting one's attention. If one allows this to happen one is rewarded by the surprising richness of aspects and facets which the painting has to offer. For instance, once one has become aware of the colour organisation which you have described so beautifully, the grandeur of the spatial display becomes apparent. The cross of the quarters which is pinpointed by the highlight on the crater draws one's attention to the off-centre position of Pan, revealing the crucial role of the vertical plumb-line. From its base, close to the satirical mask at the bottom, a kind of V-shape opens up which encompasses the core of the painting, setting apart two triangular compartments to the left and right. These broad divisions, with approximately four or five figures in each section, act like the ribs of a big fan, unfolding in space.

BR As a comment on those diagonals Poussin drops a few small hints in the foreground to help one see the painting: the pan-pipes in sharp perspective on one side, the vase on the other. They say, in effect, look as we point – using the projective spatial reading we indicate. If one takes these hints, the two wings of the movement appear thick, deep and curving forwards.

RK It's double reading again, isn't it? The angles of perspective played against the flat diagonals of the big V. But where is the vanishing point? Behind that charming couple in the centre, the woman teasing the fallen satyr?

BR There is no literal convergence. In lieu, Poussin joins up the highly lit foreground, the central recession and the far distance in his usual contradictory fashion. They may be seen as successive steps backwards; or the selfsame passage can be perceived as nearly flat, as space stacked, so to speak, with one visual event piled upon another . . .

RK Beginning with that masterpiece of pictorial fiction: the loosely draped cloth

Fig. 10. Picasso, study after Poussin's *Triumph of Pan*, 1944

in the bottom centre, enigmatically resembling the shape of a figure.

BR It's a wonderful invention. In some ways the touchstone of the painting. So white, with its dark shadow above, it undercuts the gravity of the scene through its relationship with the clouds in the sky. It seems as though the weight of one's glance has somehow pressed this cloth, and as a result a vision has sprung up. It may still be earthbound in its rougher quarters to the left and right, but as these are drawn back into shade the more delicate centre floats free, suspended, almost levitating above the ground below.

RK In other words: Poussin articulates, with the greatest possible formality, the very opposite of construction and detachment – the state of ecstasy. It must have been this artistic magic, the squaring of the circle, so to speak, that attracted Picasso. In August 1944, during the liberation of Paris when people were dancing in the streets, he celebrated the event in his own, inimitable way. He shut himself up in his studio and painted two versions after the *Triumph of Pan* – 'pour me discipliner', he said. Isn't it remarkable that a painter so alien to us as Poussin seems to be should appeal to a modern artist?

BR It's Picasso's temperament. He was probably the only modern painter who could act out the tradition again, even if it was only as a mask. You have to be a very good impersonator to play those roles. But there is a different connection to the past, and especially to Poussin. He's not really so strange as his complex imagery might suggest.

RK One wonders, anyway, what his imagery means – outside the painting. Although it is certainly not yet a mask, there is a lot in what you have said about the white cloth in the foreground of the *Triumph of Pan*. Poussin has merged several Antique sources: the worship of Pan with that of Priapus, the god of the garden, and both these fertility cults with that of Bacchus. It seems as if he has attempted a sort of composite mythology, saying in what could be called the perfect tense of painting: 'Look, this world *has been* – and therefore still *is*, though only in the imaginative presence of the artefact.' The *Triumph of Pan* concludes in a way the legend of mythological painting which Titian began. Poussin was the last of those painters of whom Cézanne could say that 'they made the sap circulate again in all those dead trees.'

BR Mythology *per se* may be finished, but something much more important, the splendour of that painting, was carried on. One only has to take Cézanne by his own declaration to see the way opening up. Take real trees, nature – Poussin's background so to speak.

RK   To make the sap of *painting* circulate again?

BR   Yes. Cézanne places his composition, *The Bathers*, firmly *in* nature and in that new context he remakes the tradition all over again.

RK   'Poussin before nature', as Bernard reports him to have said. But surely this does not mean that he painted *The Bathers* after nature?

BR   No, they are clearly not painted in terms of natural reality, or verisimilitude, but they are treated as part of nature in a very special sense. They seem to be built up out of the sensations nature provides. The bodies are like rocks, or clouds; limbs suggest branches. In working *sur le motif* Cézanne realised that light, reflections and shadows dematerialise the objects to such a point that they become malleable and can be refabricated. The *harmonie générale*, the unity of colour, to which he often refers, provides the building material for this refabrication. But this harmony is not a physical fact, readily available: it is a labyrinth of relationships to which perception opens the door.

RK   And what one sees appears at first crude and coarse. What Cézanne calls a 'harmony' can be a shock.

BR   Yes, comparable only to that encountered in the Titian. In *Bacchus and Ariadne* it is the power of blue pitched against the narrative, a tension between perception and conception. In *The Bathers* perception is held by a different reality – *paint*, uncompromisingly so.

RK   The attention which the painting commands seems to spring from its very intransigence.

BR   Even so, there is still a surprising amount that is familiar in it. There is the entry figure and also the one which reverses the movement. Look at the contrasts, echoes and modulations in both form and colour; the presence of a colour envelope and, of course, the diagonals.

RK   I agree, the affinities are striking, and yet . . . the thinking seems to be quite different. For instance, the use of diagonals bears no resemblance to that in any of the other paintings.

BR   It seems that they have a wide range of functions. Although there are major diagonals in the trees and figures, none completely bisects the area or determines orientation. None leads a progressive movement. But they

7. Cézanne, *The Bathers,* exhibited 1907

contribute both to divisions within the canvas and to the interplay of rhythms. The entire surface is charged with forces, meshed in an angular fabric of extraordinary muscularity. Thrusts are pitched one against the other, even the brushmarks have a directional pull. Through a multiplicity of diagonals Cézanne builds up a highly sensitive visual field which allows him to accumulate and disperse tensions, to shift changing rhythms through the painting.

RK   The coherence is, as you say, quite extraordinary. Each place in the canvas has its own character, and although all of them are mutually interrelated, the particular unity which emerges doesn't seem to absorb these distinctions – its amazing firmness depends rather on the capacity to retain individual frictions. This is an unprecedented way of setting about 'order' in painting. But it is interesting that it seems to be restricted to Cézanne's oil paintings. In his watercolours he aims much more, as Poussin did in his ink drawings, at an overriding rhythm.

Fig. 11. Cézanne, *Bathers,*
watercolour, 1902–6

BR   Like Poussin, Cézanne also uses his colour to qualify rhythm. But more to the point, he makes it – perhaps again like Poussin, though in a different sense – substantiate his vision. The palette is introduced through the girl and tree on the left, a composite configuration on many levels. Tonally they state extremes of contrast, formally one entity – her back leg plants the line of the tree trunk firmly on the ground, her head merges into the bark. Jointly, these two present the colour harmony of the painting – in the tints of the body, in the shades of vegetation. It consists of ochres, blues, pinks, greens and whites – derivatives of earth, skin, sky, sunlight, leaves and opalescent clouds.

RK   So it is one collective colour bracket which is distinguished mainly through tone and the emphasis which its actual placement suggests?

BR   Yes. To put it as simply as possible: Cézanne takes his group of colours and works his painting with all of them together. They may be present in a light area or in a dark one. In either case the tonal pitch of the whole group will be affected. The same area will also be predominantly one of these colours, with all the others modifying it in turn. For instance, see the body of the woman lying on the ground. Ochre sets the key at a certain tonal pitch; greens, pinks, blues and even the whites are adjusted, broadly speaking, to this pitch; and together they play through the body. Quite clearly their main role is not one of

41

describing the form, or of turning it in space. In fact, they are deliberately placed in such a way that it is impossible to read them like that, as one can in a Rubens for instance. Their dislocation sets them free to be perceived in their own terms, as colours, and to be re-related as a harmony, shifting its internal relationships inch by inch.

RK This means, if I understand rightly, that there is no particular area in the painting where the colour harmony is fully explained, or could be seen at its most prominent, as it was in the complexion of skin with Rubens. Cézanne develops his group of colours with an ever-changing bias throughout the painting, displaying one tendency here, another there.

BR It is what he called *moduler*. There are no 'boundaries' in Cézanne's way of drawing with colour. He may use lines but not for any delineation or confining of a form. The beautiful backs of the two young girls turned towards the sky are built up of parallel strokes of colour which include the back of the woman lying down, the drapery, and the leg of an adjacent figure in one rhythmic entity. The dominant white turns this passage into a subtle variant of the cloud colour above. The broad strokes of white-blues, white-greens, white-pinks and white-ochres reappear, more closely related. Cézanne modulates them by dividing the principal hues. So, across these backs, the blues include a variety of warm and cold shades; the greens, turquoises and olives; the pinks, lilacs and ochres.

RK This could sound very mechanical, as if a set of chosen colours is methodically broken down into its possible derivatives . . .

BR Do you think so? It's actually how nature herself operates. Cézanne knew this. He had seen for himself, out there in the open air, that all colours are present in any given situation, though of course in different proportions, strengths and tones. The sensation produced by that 'mechanical' handling of colours in those backs we have been talking about is one of luminous light. When he tackles a dark area, he resorts to the same technique. Take the tree trunks and foliage on the extreme left. The whites are opened up to a range of subtly tinted greys. The blues gain intensity and depth but still operate as a scale of warm to cold. The greens include strong variants of olive and turquoise. The reds are reduced to some low-key violets and browns. The yellows almost disappear, just a very few traces of yellow green remain. Fundamentally it's the same, it's only – and an all-important *only* – that the sensation Cézanne re-creates in each instance through his palette is the particular balance of the unity of colour.

RK Which Veronese had understood imaginatively.

BR Cézanne proves it. The sensation of the standing stone-like woman in the shadow of the entry figure requires that he reduce this same palette and, keying it into the sky, makes this presence almost transparent by a few touches of ochres and strong greens. It's a rebalancing of his general harmony in response to a sensation which – if not actually seen and painted *vis-à-vis* – has been perceived, assimilated, analysed and recalled.

RK And yet, one question still remains. Cézanne's 'logic of organised sensations' may be fully convincing, and in the meantime even widely accepted by the public, when it is applied to still lifes or to the Montagne Sainte-Victoire. But with a painting reminiscent of such a grand iconographic tradition, one issue begs questioning: Who are these figures? If they do not resemble any women we know, what do they represent?

BR One cannot say who they are in any literal sense, or what they may represent with any certainty. But one thing is clear, they belong to a *place* – a place best described as Cézanne described it: through colour.

RK You mean that these figures are located, within the modulations of the painting, precisely between the cool blue-and-white dominance of the sky and the warm green-and-ochre tendency of the earth colours?

BR Yes, they are. But more important, it seems to me, is a shift of context, the basic tone of the painting. It's all about blue. The blue of Titian is that of infinity, a quality which is essentially 'over there', to which mortals may relate by contrast and to which the god-like can connect through divine gestures. But Cézanne's blue encompasses us and all things in an entire range of vision. It spans from the most fugitive inflections to the impenetrable volume of the sky.

RK But it does not lose anything of its remoteness, despite coming up so close in front and virtually radiating out from the painting. Cézanne's blue seems to be the perfect envelope for the enigmatic rapport among his figures. They are overtly turned away from us, with one significant exception, pin-pointing this attitude. Although there is no contact between the figures, apart from the continuous web of colour, the whole assembly is quietly pulled together towards an inexplicit goal.

BR   Painters have always needed a sort of veil upon which they can focus their direct attention. It's as though the more fully the consciousness is absorbed, the greater the freedom of the spirit behind. In the tradition an important aspect of this veil was given by mythology and the Bible. If these spiritual perspectives are no longer available, the alternative is not plain realism. At the most, the painter may be led through the pursuit of his art, like Cézanne was, to 'realise' the veil of reality as such.

Fig. 12. Picasso, study for *Bathers in the Wood*, 1908

RK   This is an endeavour of a very high order, but perhaps the quintessence of modern art. It may explain why both Picasso and Matisse had a special love for Cézanne's late *Bathers*. In 1908, on the threshold of Cubism, Picasso worked on a group of related images which finally led to the famous *Three Women*; and Matisse bought as early as 1899 Cézanne's *Three Bathers*, which he kept with him, as a kind of talisman, for almost forty years, until he gave it away to a museum. But they were both figurative artists. How does an abstract artist relate to this past?

BR   Simply by looking. There can be no other viable relationship to history for a painter today. As modern artists we are not supported by any tradition that provides a reliable context of working, but we can appreciate, as nobody ever could before, the privilege of looking at the achievements of art as a whole.

RK   And perhaps find out that these artists also looked at each other, at least those which you have selected. In our discussion I have become very much aware that the title of this exhibition has yet another meaning . . .

BR   They may be artists whom I have selected at the moment, but they have selected each other through their work; and as much as we have enjoyed looking at them, I cannot forget that these paintings, however long ago they were made, unavoidably exert a judgement simply through their presence. It's almost as though one were being watched by them.

Paintings selected by Bridget Riley

PLATE 1
Titian (active before 1511, died 1576)
Bacchus and Ariadne, 1520–2
Canvas, 175.2 × 190.5 cm

PLATE 2
Paolo Veronese (1528?–1588)
The Adoration of the Kings, 1573
Canvas, 355.6 × 320 cm

PLATE 3
El Greco (1541–1614)
*The Expulsion of the Traders from the Temple, c. 1600
(Christ driving the Traders from the Temple)*
Canvas, 106.3 × 129.7 cm

PLATE 4
Peter Paul Rubens (1577–1640)
Allegory of Peace ('Peace and War'), 1629–30
Canvas, 203.5 × 298 cm

PLATE 5
Nicolas Poussin (1594?–1665)
The Adoration of the Shepherds, c. 1637
Canvas, 96.5 × 73.7 cm

PLATE 6
Nicolas Poussin (1594?–1665)
The Triumph of Pan, before 1636
Canvas, 134 × 145 cm

PLATE 7
Paul Cézanne (1839–1906)
The Bathers (Les Grandes Baigneuses)
Exhibited 1907
Canvas, 127.2 × 196.1 cm

List of Figures

FIG. 10
Pablo Picasso (1881–1973)
Study after Poussin's *Triumph of Pan*
Watercolour and coloured gouache on paper,
30.5 × 40.5 cm
Zervos, XIV, p. 23, no. 35
Present location unknown
© DACS 1989
Photo: Cahiers d'Art

FIG. 11
Paul Cézanne (1839–1906)
Bathers
Watercolour on buff-coloured leaf from a
sketchbook, 21 × 27 cm
Venturi 1111
Private collection
Photo: Foto-Studio H. Humm, Zurich

FIG. 12
Pablo Picasso (1881–1973)
Study for *Bathers in the Wood*
Charcoal on paper, 47.7 × 60.2 cm
Paris, Musée Picasso
© DACS 1989
Photo: Réunion des musées nationaux